BLASTED BY BLIZZARDS

JILL KEPPELER

PowerKiDS
press
New York

Published in 2018 by The Rosen Publishing Group, Inc.
29 East 21st Street, New York, NY 10010

First Edition

Editor: Melissa Raé Shofner
Book Design: Reann Nye

Photo Credits: Cover, p. 1 Uriel Sinai/Getty Images Europe/Getty Images; pp. 4–30 (background) Aleksey Stemmer/Shutterstock.com; p. 4 Mariami Aphkhazava/Shutterstock.com; p. 5 Gadelshina Dina/Shutterstock.com; p. 6 Courtesy of the Library of Congress; pp. 9, 17, 23 John Normile/Getty Images News/Getty Images; p. 11 Pasha_Barabanov/Shutterstock.com; p. 13 Photo Researchers/Science Source/Getty Images; p. 15 lpedan/Shutterstock.com; p. 16 Andriy Blokhin/Shutterstock.com; p. 19 LindaRaymondPhotography/Moment/Getty Images; p. 20 Dmitry Kalinovsky/Shutterstock.com; p. 21 bibiphoto/Shutterstock.com; p. 22 Maryna Pleshkun/Shutterstock.com; p. 24 Maxim Blinkov/Shutterstock.com; p. 25 Spok83/Shutterstock.com; p. 27 stephanie zell/Moment/Getty Images; p. 29 Johannes Simon/Getty Images News/Getty Images.

Library of Congress Cataloging-in-Publication Data

Names: Keppeler, Jill, author.
Title: Blasted by blizzards / Jill Keppeler.
Description: New York : PowerKids Press, [2018] | Series: Natural disasters: how people survive | Includes index.
Identifiers: LCCN 2017025256| ISBN 9781538325599 (library bound) | ISBN 9781538326282 (pbk.) | ISBN 9781538326299 (6 pack)
Subjects: LCSH: Blizzards–Juvenile literature.
Classification: LCC QC926.37 .K47 2018 | DDC 363.34/625–dc23
LC record available at https://lccn.loc.gov/2017025256

Manufactured in the United States of America

CPSIA Compliance Information: Batch #BW18PK: For Further Information contact Rosen Publishing, New York, New York at 1-800-237-9932

CONTENTS

DISASTER STRIKES!

Snow can be a lot of fun. You can build a snowman, have a snowball fight, or go sledding on this fluffy white stuff that falls from the sky. Some days, you might even get a day off from school if it snows too much!

But snow can have a dark side, too. If too much snow falls too quickly and is combined with other weather events, a snowstorm can become a blizzard. A blizzard is

DISASTER ALERT!

Snow often looks white and fluffy, but it's made of ice crystals. We usually think of crystals as rocks, but ice crystals are made of frozen water.

Snow can be a lot of fun, but too much snow at once can cause a lot of trouble.

a type of natural disaster, or a sudden natural event that can cause a lot of damage. Natural disasters can also cause many deaths.

Luckily, people have learned many ways to deal with and survive natural disasters, including blizzards. Read on to learn more about how to stay safe during a blizzard!

WHAT MAKES A BLIZZARD?

Many people think any big snowstorm is a blizzard. However, this isn't true! To be a blizzard, a storm must have strong winds and snow that is falling or blowing. These conditions must last for at least three hours, and the winds must be blowing at least 35 miles (56.3 km) per hour.

A blizzard must also cause poor visibility for people. If you're out in a blizzard, you won't be able to see more than a quarter mile (0.4 km) ahead of you. Sometimes, you'll be able to see much less. This is one of the reasons blizzards are so dangerous. They can cause car accidents, and people can get lost very easily.

Snow is shown blowing nearly sideways in this photograph taken during the Great Blizzard of 1888 in New York City.

HISTORIC U.S. BLIZZARDS

The Great Blizzard of 1888

when: March 11 and 12, 1888
where: Connecticut, Massachusetts,
   New Jersey, New York, and Rhode Island
death toll: more than 400 people
amount of snow: 40 to 50 inches

The Great Blizzard of 1899

when: February 11, 1899
where: Georgia to Maine
death toll: more than 100 people
amount of snow: up to 34 inches

The Great Appalachian Storm

when: November 24, 1950
where: Appalachian area of the United States and
   into Canada
death toll: more than 350 people
amount of snow: more than 57 inches

The Storm of the Century

when: March 12, 1993
where: much of the United States, ranged
   Cuba to Canada
death toll: about 310 people
amount of snow: up to 60 inches

For a blizzard to form, it needs to be cold, both on the ground and higher in Earth's atmosphere. Water freezes at 32° Fahrenheit (0° Celsius). If water **condenses** in the air at that temperature, it can freeze into ice crystals and become snow. The temperature on the ground must usually be 41° Fahrenheit (5° Celsius) or lower for the snow to reach it.

Wind, the other part of a blizzard, is moving air. Air flows from areas of high pressure in the atmosphere to areas of low pressure. The closer the high-pressure areas are to the low-pressure areas, the stronger the wind will be.

When all these things—water in the atmosphere, cold temperatures, and strong winds—come together, there might be a blizzard!

DISASTER ALERT!

It can be too warm to snow, but it can't be too cold to snow. However, it snows most often when the temperature near the ground is 15° Fahrenheit (-9° Celsius) or warmer.

A car is shown partially buried by snow after a lake-effect storm in November 2014 in Buffalo, New York. The storm dropped nearly 7 feet (2.1 m) of snow in some places!

Lake-Effect Snow

Lake-effect snow happens when cold air moves over the warmer waters of a lake. This chilly air picks up warm water vapor, which rises, cools, and forms narrow bands of clouds. These clouds can produce 2 to 3 inches (5 to 7.6 cm) of snow per hour—or more! Wind direction determines which areas will be hit with lake-effect snow. Because the snow bands are narrow, it may be snowing heavily in one and sunny just a few miles away!

SNOW COUNTRY

Some places on Earth are more likely to get blizzards than others. The conditions must be right for snow and wind. In the United States, this is most common in the Great Plains and Upper Midwest, but blizzards can happen almost anywhere in the country. They're least likely to happen in the warm Gulf Coast (which includes the states bordering the Gulf of Mexico) and the coast of California.

Blizzard Alley is an area in the Great Plains that tends to have the highest concentration of blizzards anywhere in the United States. It includes the states of North and South Dakota and western Minnesota. These areas have flat land with few trees, which means there's not much there to lessen cold winds blowing south from Canada.

DISASTER ALERT!

A study in 2002 used scientific data from October 1959 to May 2000 to show where most blizzards take place in the United States. Traill County in eastern North Dakota won the prize, with 74 blizzards in nearly 41 years.

Areas around Blizzard Alley may also get more blizzards than the rest of the United States. This includes the rest of Minnesota and parts of Iowa, Nebraska, Kansas, Colorado, Wyoming, and Idaho.

BLIZZARD ALLEY

NORTH DAKOTA

MINNESOTA

SOUTH DAKOTA

WYOMING

IOWA

NEBRASKA

NUMBER OF BLIZZARDS
(1959–2000)

41–74

21–40

11–20

COLORADO

KANSAS

Cold Conditions

Blizzards can take place all over the world, even in **tropical** areas! Warm areas of Earth can have cold mountaintops where blizzards can form. They're most common, though, in Russia and Canada. Some very cold areas rarely get snow or blizzards at all. The Dry Valleys in Antarctica are very cold but have very low humidity. That means there's little water in the air to form snow.

PREDICTING A STORM

Blizzards can be very dangerous, so it's important to know if one is heading your way. Meteorologists, or people who study weather, **climate**, and the atmosphere, keep a close eye on weather conditions so they can warn us if a blizzard is on the way.

These scientists use a number of tools to help them watch weather patterns and **predict** what's coming. They study weather conditions that took place in the past and use that information to forecast what might happen in the future. Computer programs help meteorologists create models of weather systems to make their predictions.

However, it's important to remember that storms can be tough to predict. The weather is always changing. Scientists must study models, patterns, and conditions carefully to make a good forecast.

DISASTER ALERT!

Meteorologists use **satellites** to keep track of weather patterns and **radar** to measure rain or snow. Computers use this information to create models of weather systems.

Sometimes meteorologists will predict a storm or blizzard for an area, but conditions may not get that bad. It can be hard to predict the weather, but it's always good to be prepared.

Prediction Puzzle

Predicting snow can be very tricky. Sometimes the worst snow can fall in very narrow bands—so narrow that they can be hard for watchers to see and predict. Also, only a few degrees of temperature can mean the difference between rain and snow. Heavy rain can create many problems, but not the same sort of problems a blizzard can create! Some forecasters say snow is the most difficult type of weather to predict.

ISSUING A WARNING

If it looks like dangerous weather may be on the way, the National Weather Service (NWS) will first note this in its **Hazardous** Weather Outlook. These predictions are made three to seven days in advance and may be uncertain.

About 24 to 72 hours ahead of time, the NWS may issue a blizzard watch. This means there's a 50 percent to 80 percent chance a blizzard will occur. People can start getting ready.

If a blizzard is imminent, or expected in the next 12 to 36 hours, the NWS will issue a blizzard warning. This means a blizzard could hit very soon or that there's a very high (80 percent or better) chance of one hitting in that time period.

DISASTER ALERT!

The National Weather Service is an **agency** of the federal government. It provides forecasts and weather, water, and climate information. It also issues warnings to help keep people safe.

A Different Sort of Blizzard

Snow doesn't have to be falling from the sky to make a blizzard.
A ground blizzard occurs when strong winds pick up snow that's
already on the ground and whip it through the air, reducing the
distance people can see. Both kinds of blizzards can also cause
drifting snow. That means the wind pushes snow into deep slopes
called drifts. It may be very deep in places. Snow drifts can bury
cars and more. They can even partly bury houses!

15

GETTING READY

If a blizzard might be on its way, there are ways to prepare for it. It's good to have an **emergency** supply kit ready. This can be helpful for many kinds of weather issues or natural disasters. A basic kit should include bottled water, food, medicines, a battery-powered radio, flashlights, and extra batteries. For winter, you can add rock salt (to melt ice on walkways), a snow shovel, and extra clothing and blankets to help you keep warm.

DISASTER ALERT!

There are many ways to stay up to date during an emergency like a blizzard. There are smartphone apps to provide weather information and apps that can help you find assistance if you need shelter or first aid.

It's important to be sure your home is ready for winter emergencies, too. This can mean having an expert check the heating system every year and being sure the roof, walls, and windows are in good shape.

You should also create a family communications plan, just in case your family members get separated during an emergency. Know how you'll contact each other and how you'll get back together.

Listen to the radio or watch TV to stay **informed** about warnings or watches. Keep cell phones charged in case the power goes out.

SAFE AND WARM

The most important thing to do during a blizzard is to stay indoors. Visibility can be bad, so you can get lost even a short distance from your home. With low temperatures and wind chills, this could be very dangerous. Listen to the radio or watch television if possible so you're informed about the storm's progress.

Even when you're inside, you may have to **conserve** the fuel used to heat your home. To keep warm, wear layers of loose-fitting, lightweight clothing. Make sure you eat regularly. Food is fuel for your body and helps keep you warm.

If you have to step outside at all, be sure you're wearing warm, waterproof clothing, including a hat and gloves. Keep dry and be careful while walking. It may be slippery!

DISASTER ALERT!

Wind chill is how cold strong winds plus low temperatures feel on bare skin. A low wind chill can be a big problem!

If you have pets, make sure they're inside during blizzards or winter storms, too!

Hypothermia and Frostbite

People who are out in very cold conditions must watch out for hypothermia and frostbite. Hypothermia is when a person's body temperature gets dangerously low. Signs include uncontrollable shivering, **numbness**, confusion, and great sleepiness. Frostbite is when a person's skin or the flesh right below it freezes. Signs include loss of feeling in these areas and cold, discolored skin. If someone has these signs, it's important to warm them up and get them medical help as soon as possible.

19

ON THE
ROAD

Although it's best to stay home during a blizzard, sometimes people get caught out in one. That's why it's a good idea to have an emergency kit in your family's car, too. This kit should have many of the same things that are in your home's kit, plus a windshield scraper and extra blankets.

It's important to keep an eye on the news during a blizzard. Sometimes roads will be closed due to snowy

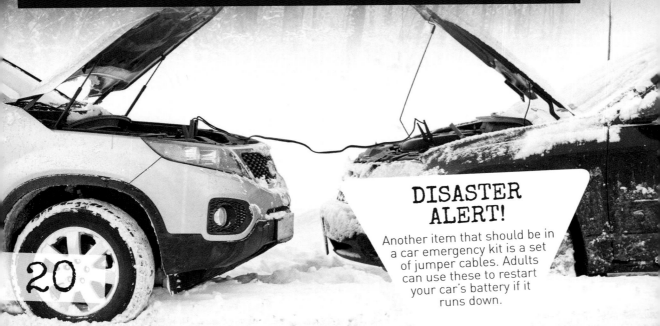

DISASTER ALERT!

Another item that should be in a car emergency kit is a set of jumper cables. Adults can use these to restart your car's battery if it runs down.

Driving in snow can be tough! You might run into a whiteout. That means visibility is nearly zero.

conditions. Officials may issue driving advisories or bans. This means you should definitely stay home!

　　If your car does get stuck in a blizzard, you should stay where you are and call or wait for help. No one should leave the car unless help is visible within about 300 feet (91.4 m) or they might get lost in blowing snow!

SNOW PROBLEMS

Although the amount of snow doesn't make a blizzard, a lot of snow can still fall during one. This can cause problems beyond the issues of poor visibility and freezing temperatures.

There are different kinds of snow, and some of them can be very wet and heavy. Snow can weigh anywhere

DISASTER ALERT!

It's a good idea to check on friends, neighbors, and relatives during emergencies such as a blizzard, especially if they're very old or live alone. It's always good to help each other.

While your family might have to clean snow off your roof for safety's sake, standing on the roof might not be the best way to do it. It's easy to fall. A snow rake lets people stand on the ground and still clear snow.

from 7 pounds (3.2 kg) per 1 cubic foot (0.03 cubic m) to 20 pounds (9.1 kg) per cubic foot. Snow that collects on tree branches can cause them to break and crash to the ground. Too much heavy snow on a building's roof can cause it to collapse. This is one reason most homes in cold, snowy areas don't have flat roofs. Snow, ice, and water can't slide off flat roofs, so they're more likely to collapse under the weight.

OTHER DANGERS

While car accidents and getting stuck in snow are reasons people are hurt or killed during and after blizzards, there are other dangers as well.

People must be careful when shoveling snow, especially very heavy snow. It's a lot of exercise! Sometimes people get hurt while shoveling. Older people may even have a heart attack. It's important to be even more careful if you have any health problems.

DISASTER ALERT!

According to a 2015 study, 571 people in the United States died because of winter storms from 1996 to 2011. If you add in the number of deaths in car and airplane crashes caused by these storms, the toll jumps to 13,852 deaths!

Carbon monoxide is also produced by some kinds of generators, which are machines people use to provide electricity for their homes if the power is out. Never use a gasoline-powered generator inside!

Carbon monoxide is another danger during a blizzard. This is a colorless, odorless gas that's very toxic. It's produced by a number of things people may use to keep warm, such as some types of stoves and grills that use gasoline, a kind of fuel. It's important to never use these things to heat your home and to have a working carbon monoxide detector.

WHAT A MESS!

Once a blizzard is over, the problems might be just beginning. There's usually a lot to clean up after a blizzard. There may be a lot of snow. Buildings may be in bad shape because of it, and power lines may be down. People may be trapped in their homes, businesses, and schools.

Cars might be stuck on roads that need to be cleared. Cities where people are used to dealing with snow may be able to send out many snowplows to clean up. If a city isn't used to snow, this might be an even bigger problem!

If there's too much snow, communities might start running out of places to put it. And when all the snow starts to melt, there may be floods.

DISASTER ALERT!

The city of Boston, Massachusetts, where it snows regularly, has about 500 snowplows. However, the city of Atlanta, Georgia, where snow is rare, has only about 70 snowplows.

In 2014, a snowstorm in Atlanta, Georgia, caused a lot of problems. Atlanta doesn't get much snow. Even a little snow in a southern city may cause more problems than a full blizzard can cause in a city where people are used to it.

THE FUTURE OF BLIZZARDS

Blizzards can be messy, expensive, and dangerous, but they're a part of life in many areas. However, scientists think that blizzards and other winter storms may become worse—and more and more common—due to climate change.

Climate change, which is a change in Earth's weather often caused by human activity, can lead to warmer weather. This means winters may get shorter, but there's more water in the air as oceans get warmer. More water in the air will mean more snow when the temperature is cold enough.

Cities and other communities may have to get even more used to dealing with big, bad blizzards as climate change continues and gets worse. Are you prepared to survive a blizzard? Stay informed, be prepared, and keep safe!

DISASTER ALERT!

The Weather Channel started naming winter storms in 2012. Some of the names have been Juno, Leo, and Athena.

Even as Earth's temperatures go up, winter storms and blizzards may increase. Climate change affects many types of weather.

BLIZZARD SAFETY TIPS

The danger isn't over after a blizzard. Follow these tips to stay safe:

-Stay inside during a blizzard if it's at all possible.

-Keep an emergency kit in your home and in your family's car. Kits should include water, food, blankets, warm clothes, shovels, batteries, a radio, and more.

-If you must go out, dress warmly and wear a hat, gloves, and boots. Don't go far.

-Avoid driving if possible.

-If your car gets stuck in a blizzard, stay inside the car unless you know help is very close.

-Listen to the radio and watch the news. Stay informed about what kind of weather is coming, how bad it's expected to be, and when it's supposed to start and end.

-Have an emergency plan with your family. Know where everyone is expected to be and when.

-Don't use gasoline-powered grills or generators inside your house.

-Make sure you have a working carbon monoxide detector.

GLOSSARY

agency: A government department that is responsible for a certain activity or area.

climate: The average weather conditions of a place over a period of time.

condense: To lose heat and change from a gas into a liquid.

conserve: To keep something from harm and not waste it.

emergency: An unexpected situation that needs quick action.

hazardous: Dangerous.

informed: Having knowledge about something.

numbness: Having no feeling.

predict: To guess what will happen in the future based on facts or knowledge.

radar: A machine that uses radio waves to locate and identify objects.

satellite: A spacecraft placed in orbit around Earth, a moon, or a planet to collect information or for communication.

tropical: Having to do with an area of the world known for warm and wet weather.

INDEX

WEBSITES

Due to the changing nature of Internet links, PowerKids Press has developed an online list of websites related to the subject of this book. This site is updated regularly. Please use this link to access the list: www.powerkidslinks.com/natd/bliz